Artistic Luxury

FABERGÉ, TIFFANY, AND THEIR CONTEMPORARIES

Pomegranate

SAN FRANCISCO

Pomegranate Communications, Inc.
Box 808022, Petaluma CA 94975
800 227 1428; www.pomegranate.com

Pomegranate Europe Ltd.
Unit 1, Heathcote Business Centre, Hurlbutt Road
Warwick, Warwickshire CV34 6TD, UK
[+44] 0 1926 430111; sales@pomeurope.co.uk

ISBN 978-0-7649-4806-0
Pomegranate Catalog No. AA578

Pomegranate publishes books of postcards on a wide range of subjects.
Please contact the publisher for more information.

Cover designed by Gina Bostian
Printed in Korea
17 16 15 14 13 12 11 10 09 08   10 9 8 7 6 5 4 3 2 1

To facilitate detachment of the postcards from this book, fold each card along its perforation line before tearing.

THE TWENTY-EIGHT STUNNING reproductions presented here—from the exhibition "Artistic Luxury: Fabergé, Tiffany, Lalique," organized by the Cleveland Museum of Art—offer a glimpse into the world of the rich and famous during the years leading up to World War I. The exhibition, opening in Cleveland in October 2008 and traveling to San Francisco's Palace of the Legion of Honor in January 2009, reunites the greatest masterworks of Peter Carl Fabergé (Russian, 1846–1920), Louis Comfort Tiffany (American, 1848–1933), and René Jules Lalique (French, 1860–1945) for the first time since the legendary 1900 Exposition Universelle in Paris provided a glamorous stage for all three designers to shine. This book of postcards includes brilliant works by Fabergé and Tiffany as well as eight of their illustrious contemporaries: Félix Bracquemond, Marius Hammer, André Fernand Thesmar, Meta Overbeck, Auguste Delaherche, F. Walter Lawrence, Carlo Bugatti, and Louis Aucoc.

Fabergé, Tiffany, and Lalique drew inspiration from both popular motifs of the past and new currents in design such as Art Nouveau and

Modernism. Fabergé, who catered primarily to the tastes of the Russian and British royal families, was the most conservative in design of the three. Lalique pushed the boundaries of his artistry toward the avant-garde and attracted the patronage of influential members of the artistic and literary circles. Tiffany had the broadest range of customers and gained a reputation for providing the most extraordinary objects of personal adornment. All three are credited with the elevation of indigenous multicolored gemstones, in opposition to the profusion of white diamonds and pearls favored by the world's aristocracy and those who emulated them.

Although the three designers competed for the same commissions and customers, they were united by a common purpose: to provide the most luxurious and artistic creations to their clientele. Their work became the ultimate status symbols of the Gilded Age.

Artistic Luxury
FABERGÉ · TIFFANY · LALIQUE

Tiffany Studios
Louis Comfort Tiffany (American, 1848–1933),
designer; Tiffany & Company, maker
Necklace, c. 1912

Gold (18 karat, cast and chased), nephrite beads
L. 34.3 cm (13½ in.), w. 8.6 cm (3⅜ in.)
Toledo Museum of Art, Purchased with funds
given by Rita Barbour Kern, 1996.1
Photograph by Tim Thayer

707 782 9000   WWW.POMEGRANATE.COM

Pomegranate

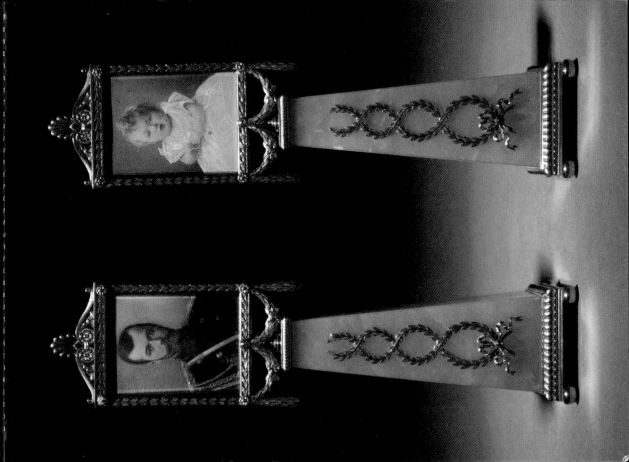

FABERGÉ · TIFFANY · LALIQUE

House of Fabergé
Framed Miniatures, before 1896

Gold, jade, rubies, gouache, ivory, glass
Overall h. 15.3 cm (6 in.), w. 5 cm (2 in.), d. 5 cm (2 in.)
Portrait of Czar Nicholas II (1966.458.1)
Portrait of Grand Duchess Olga (1966.458.2)
The Cleveland Museum of Art,
The India Early Minshall Collection

707 782 9000   WWW.POMEGRANATE.COM

Pomegranate

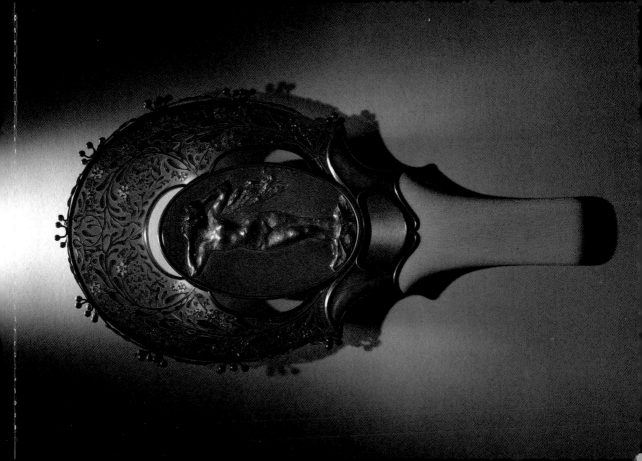

Pomegranate

707 782 9000   WWW.POMEGRANATE.COM

Artistic Luxury
FABERGÉ · TIFFANY · LALIQUE

Marius Hammer (Norwegian, 1847–1912)
Vase, 1900–1910

Enamel, plique-à-jour technique; silver, soldered and gilded
H. 21.6 cm (8½ in.)
Toledo Museum of Art, Purchased with funds
from the Libbey Endowment,
Gift of Edward Drummond Libbey, 2006.16
Photograph by Toni Marie Gonzalez

André Fernand Thesmar (French, 1843–1912)
Bowl with Anemones, 1900

Gold; translucent enamel, plique-à-jour technique
H. 5 cm (2 in.), diam. (rim) 9.1 cm (3⅝ in.)
Toledo Museum of Art,
Mr. and Mrs. George M. Jones, Jr. Fund, 2005.43
Photograph by Toni Marie Gonzalez

707 782 9000   WWW.POMEGRANATE.COM

Pomegranate

FABERGÉ · TIFFANY · LALIQUE

House of Fabergé
Tea Service and Tea Table, 1896–1908

Table: lemonwood, silver and ormolu mounts,
Karelian birch veneer, 71.8 cm (28¼) in.
Tea service: silver, ivory, dimensions variable
Fine Arts Museums of San Francisco, Gift of Victoria Melita,
Grand Duchess Kiril, through Alma de Bretteville Spreckels,
1945.366.1 and 1945.355-65

707 782 9000   WWW.POMEGRANATE.COM

Pomegranate

House of Fabergé
Imperial Red Cross Easter Egg, 1915

Gold, silver, enamel, glass
Overall h. 8.6 cm (3⅜ in.), w. 6.4 cm (2½ in.)
The Cleveland Museum of Art,
The India Early Minshall Collection, 1963.673

Pomegranate   707 782 9000   WWW.POMEGRANATE.COM

Artistic Luxury
FABERGÉ · TIFFANY · LALIQUE

House of Fabergé
Candelabra, before 1896

Overall h. 28.5 cm (11¼ in.), w. 25.1 cm (9⅞ in.),
d. 12 cm (4¾ in.)
The Cleveland Museum of Art,
The India Early Minshall Collection, 1966.494.1-.2

707 782 9000   WWW.POMEGRANATE.COM

Pomegranate

Artistic Luxury
FABERGÉ · TIFFANY · LALIQUE

House of Fabergé
Parrot Figurine, 1903

Silver, enamel, jasper, agate, emeralds
Overall h. 15.3 cm (6 in.), w. 7.4 cm (2⅞ in.)
The Cleveland Museum of Art,
The India Early Minshall Collection, 1966.447

707 782 9000   WWW.POMEGRANATE.COM

Pomegranate

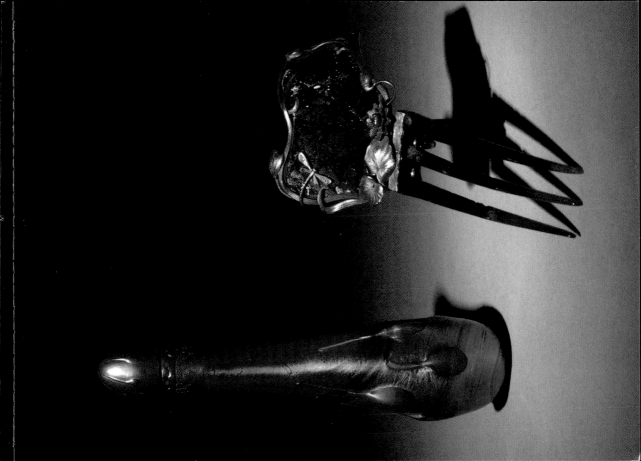

Tiffany Studios
Louis Comfort Tiffany (American, 1848–1933)
Perfume Bottle, c. 1900

Favrile glass, gilt metal
Overall h. 13.4 cm (5¼ in.)
The Cleveland Museum of Art, Gift of Ellen Wade Chinn,
Elizabeth Wade Sedgwick and J. H. Wade III in memory of
their mother, Irene Love Wade, 1966.379

F. Walter Lawrence (American, 1864–1929)
Ornamental Comb, 1890–1910

Gold, ancient glass, gemstones, tortoiseshell
Overall h. 14.3 cm (5⅝ in.), w. 5.8 cm (2¼ in.), d. 1.9 cm (¾ in.)
The Cleveland Museum of Art,
Gift of Trideca Society, 2001.106

WWW.POMEGRANATE.COM

707 782 9000

Pomegranate

House of Fabergé
Miniature Bidet, 1908–1917

Gold, silver gilt, enamel over engine-turned ground,
rubies, diamonds
Overall h. 2.9 cm (1⅛ in.), w. 11.7 cm (4⅝ in.), d. 9.9 cm (3⅞ in.)
The Cleveland Museum of Art,
The India Early Minshall Collection, 1966.455

707 782 9000   WWW.POMEGRANATE.COM

Pomegranate

Auguste Delaherche (French, 1857–1940)
Vase, c. 1895

Stoneware with silver mounts and glass beads
Overall h. 19.6 cm (7¾ in.), diam. 7.7 cm (3 in.)
The Cleveland Museum of Art,
Gift of Henry H. Hawley, 1997.288

707 782 9000   WWW.POMEGRANATE.COM

Pomegranate

House of Fabergé
Tea Set, before 1896

Silver gilt, enamel, various dimensions
The Cleveland Museum of Art,
The India Early Minshall Collection, 1966.500.1-.11

Artistic Luxury
FABERGÉ · TIFFANY · LALIQUE

Carlo Bugatti (Italian, 1856–1940)
Table, Salver, and Service, c. 1907

Table: inlaid wood, cast and gilded bronze mounts, inlays of
ivory or bone, metal, and mother-of-pearl, overall h. 71.5 cm
(28⅛ in.), w. 67.1 cm (26⅜ in.), d. 41.3 cm (16¼ in.)
Salver: silver and ivory, overall h. 14.6 cm (5¾ in.),
w. 33 cm (13 in.)
Tea service: silver and ivory, dimensions variable
The Cleveland Museum of Art, The Thomas L. Fawick
Memorial Collection, Leonard C. Hanna, Jr. Fund,
1991.45-46 (table and salver) and 1980.74.1-5 (tea service)

707 782 9000   WWW.POMEGRANATE.COM

Pomegranate

Tiffany & Company
Tankard, c. 1900

Silver, gilt, ivory
Overall h. 69.9 cm (27½ in.), w. 29.2 cm (11½ in.),
d. 33.7 cm (13¼ in.)
Tiffany & Company Archives, B2001.06
© Tiffany & Co.

707 782 9000   WWW.POMEGRANATE.COM

Pomegranate

Artistic Luxury
FABERGÉ · TIFFANY · LALIQUE

House of Fabergé
Barometer, 1896–1903

Palisander, silver gilt, garnet
Overall h. 14 cm (5½ in.), w. 12.5 cm (4¹⁵⁄₁₆ in.)
The Cleveland Museum of Art,
The India Early Minshall Collection, 1966.484

707 782 9000   WWW.POMEGRANATE.COM

Pomegranate

FABERGÉ · TIFFANY · LALIQUE

House of Fabergé
Lapis Lazuli Easter Egg, 1895–1900

Gold, enamel, lapis lazuli, pearls, diamonds, rubies
Overall h. 5.9 cm (2⁵⁄₁₆ in.), w. 4.5 cm (1¾ in.)
The Cleveland Museum of Art,
The India Early Minshall Collection, 1966.436

707 782 9000   WWW.POMEGRANATE.COM

Pomegranate

Louis Aucoc (French, 1850–1932)
Neck Plaque in the Art Nouveau Style, c. 1900

Gold, platinum, diamonds, enamel
Overall h. 4.5 cm (1¾ in.), w. 7.6 cm (3 in.)
Collection of The Newark Museum,
Gift of Herman A. E. and Paul C. Jaehne, 1941, 41.725

707 782 9000   WWW.POMEGRANATE.COM

Pomegranate

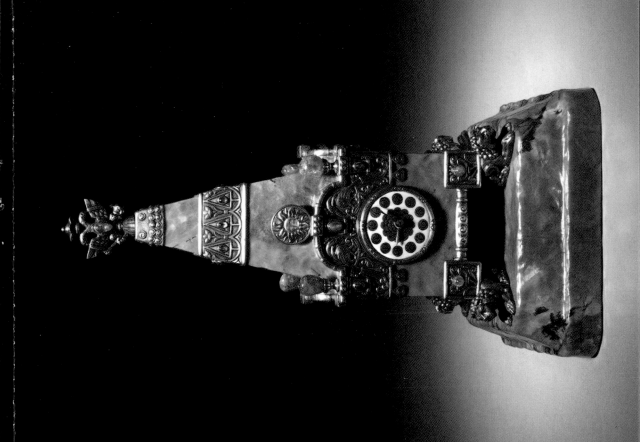

Artistic Luxury
FABERGÉ · TIFFANY · LALIQUE

House of Fabergé
Kremlin Tower Clock, 1913

Rhodonite, silver, enamel, emeralds, sapphires
Overall h. 29 cm (11⅜ in.), w. 14.6 cm (5¾ in.)
The Cleveland Museum of Art,
The India Early Minshall Collection, 1966.477

707 782 9000   WWW.POMEGRANATE.COM

Pomegranate